Hi There!

Starting a new job can be overwhelming, and it's easy to assume that you will receive adequate training from your employer. However, the reality is that not all companies prioritize employee training and development. But don't worry, you have the power to take control of your own training and development.

This companion workbook is designed to be your personal training guide, with each section corresponding to a resource covered in the Ace Your New Job book. By completing the worksheets and answering the questions, you will gain a deeper understanding of your job responsibilities, your company, and how your role fits into the bigger picture.

No matter the situation you are facing in your new role, you can choose to train yourself with the help of this workbook and the Ace Your New Job: A Guide to Training Yourself book. It's the perfect activity to tackle when you're feeling lost or unsure of where to start.

I recommend reviewing one chapter of the book and completing the corresponding section of the workbook. It's an easy and effective way to set yourself up for success and ace your new job. You've got this!

Deborah Pinnock, SHRM-CP
CEO & Founder of DebTalk, LLC

ACE YOUR NEW JOB

Table of Contents

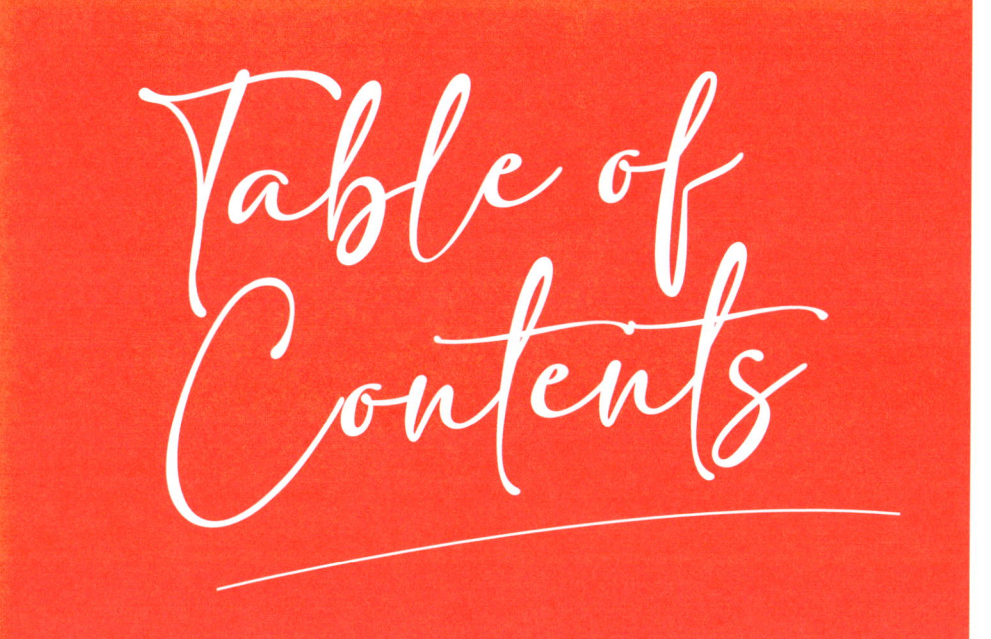

Introduction

1. The Website   4

2. The Executive Summary   6

3. The Job Description   8

4. The Organization Chart   10

5. The Annual Report   13

6. Team Interviews   19

7. Observation   26

8. Role-Related Software   31

9. E-Learning Resources   32

Self-Assessment   34

Reflections   40

1
WEBSITE WORKSHEET

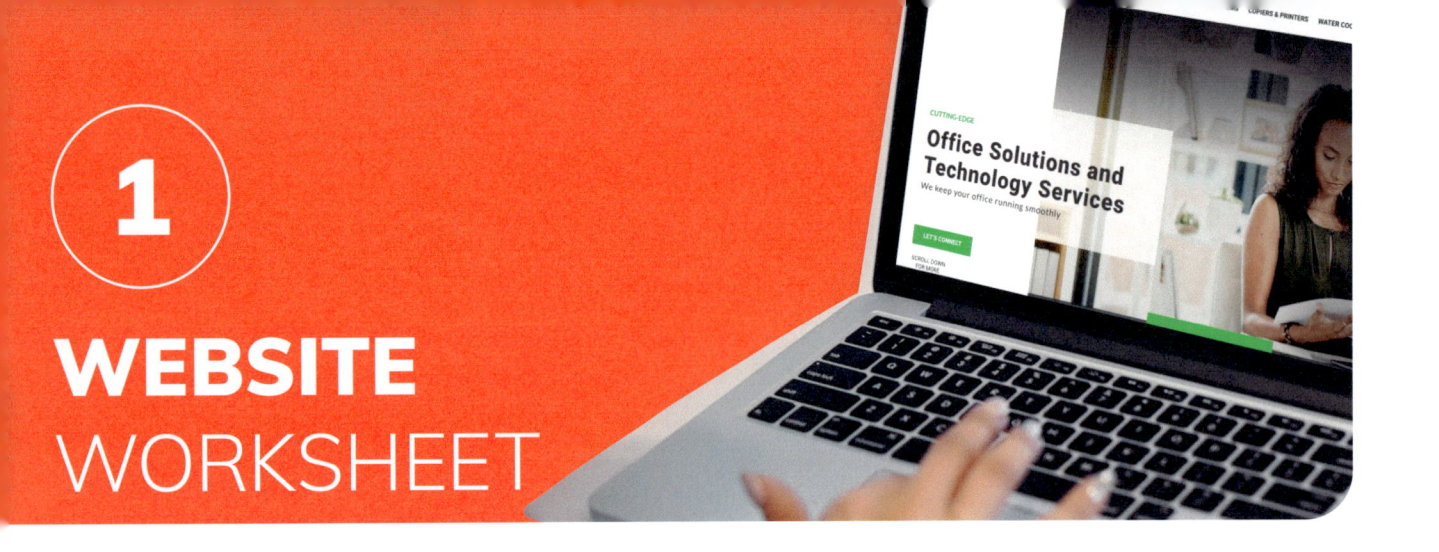

Just as people's homes reveal things about them, a company's website, its virtual home, does the same. Use the questions below to get better acquainted with your organization.

1 What is the name and mission (i.e. core purpose) of your company?

2 How long has it been in existence?

3 List the main products or services your company provides, along with any unique features that make them stand out.

    A. Product or Service Name 1

    Description & Standout Feature

    B. Product or Service Name 2

    Description & Standout Feature

ACE YOUR NEW JOB

C. Product or Service Name 3

Description & Standout Feature

D. Product or Service Name 4

Description & Standout Feature

4 Write the title and a brief summary of the three most recent press releases, media releases or company updates.

Topic

Summary

Topic

Summary

Topic

Summary

2

EXECUTIVE SUMMARY
WORKSHEET

Review the executive summary to gather information about the company's mission, its products and services, target market(s), competitors and more. Utilize this summary to answer the following questions. Note that some companies may not have an executive summary:

1 Why does the company exist?

2 Which group of people or organizations is the company trying to reach with its products and/or services?

3 What are the main products and services the company offers per the executive summary?

4 What action(s) is the company taking to market the business and the products?

ACE YOUR NEW JOB

6

5 What sales strategies are being used to advance the company's products and services?

6 Who are the company's top 3 competitors?

7 What are the top strengths of your company?

8 What are the top three weaknesses of your company?

9 What 3 things differentiate your company from its competitors?

10 List the top 3 future plans of the business.

DEBORAH PINNOCK

3 JOB DESCRIPTION WORKSHEET

The job description is vital in helping you understand the responsibilities of your role and the skills and competencies required to do it.

1 What is your title?

2 Write 3-5 sentences that provide a summary of your job. Include how it helps the organization achieve its mission.

3 List the main responsibilities of your job. Write them in order of significance.

ACE YOUR NEW JOB

4 What are the skills and qualifications that are necessary to thrive in this role? You can include personality, education, certifications, experience and more.

5 What experiences or skills do you possess that position you to thrive in this role?

6 What skill or competencies should you develop based on the "desired but not required" segment of the job description, if applicable?

DEBORAH PINNOCK

4
ORGANIZATION CHART WORKSHEET

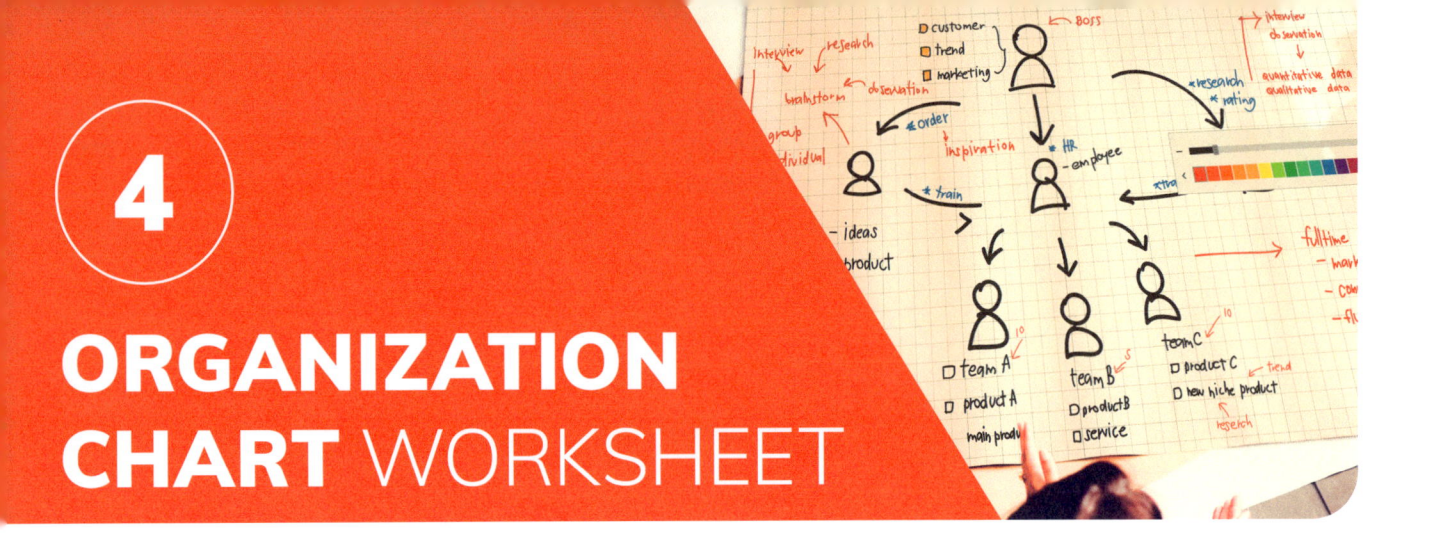

The organization chart is a visual representation of how a company is organized. It reveals the company's structure, key decision-makers, levels of authority, reporting relationships, and more. This tool also aids in identifying the individual who can assist you with various matters.

1 Who is the leader of your organization and what is the individual's title? Some examples are CEO, president, executive director, chairperson, principal, dean, founder, etc.

Name   Title

2 To whom does this person report?

3 List the names and titles of those who report to this individual.

ACE YOUR NEW JOB

4 What is the name and title of the person to whom you report? If it is a matrix organization, list all the names of your managers and their titles.

5 What are the names and titles of those who report directly to your manager?

6 What is the name and title of your manager's manager?

7 List the department(s) with which you will collaborate often.

7a. List the name of the key person from each of the departments mentioned in number 7 plus their contact information.

Name
Title
Department
Phone Number
E-mail Address

Name
Title
Department
Phone Number
E-mail Address

Name
Title
Department
Phone Number
E-mail Address

Name
Title
Department
Phone Number
E-mail Address

Name
Title
Department
Phone Number
E-mail Address

ACE YOUR NEW JOB

5 ANNUAL REPORT WORKSHEET

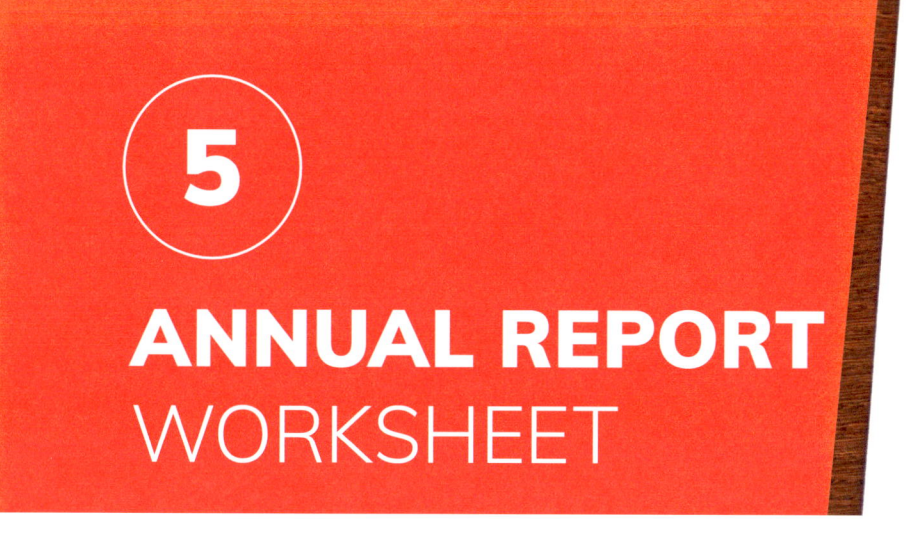

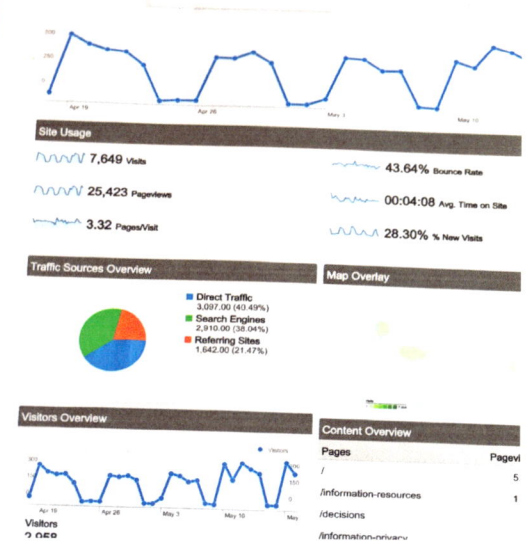

An annual report is an important document that public corporations must provide each year to shareholders describing the company's performance and financial condition. Keep in mind that private companies are generally not required to provide an annual report to the public.

1 What are the top 3 achievements or highlights listed in the annual report?

A.

B.

C.

2 Which highlight is most related to your role? Summarize it.

3 What is the gross and net income, and earnings for the current year, as well as the last two years.

Gross Income:

Year 1 (Current Year):

Year 2 (Prior Year):

Year 3 (Prior Year):

*This represents volume of product or services sold.

DEBORAH PINNOCK

Net Income:

Year 1 (Current Year):

Year 2 (Prior Year):

Year 3 (Prior Year):

*This represents the income minus the cost of directly providing the products or services.

Earnings:

Year 1 (Current Year):

Year 2 (Prior Year):

Year 3 (Prior Year):

*This represents the company profit.

Note: This information can be found on the income statement, also known as the P&L (profit and loss) statement in the financial section.

4 Briefly describe the company's strategic plan for future success.

5 What are the key areas the company uses to measure success? These are also known as key performance indicators (KPIs). They are typically found within the narrative section. Read more about KPIs here: https://www.investopedia.com/terms/k/kpi.asp

6 How does this year's performance in the key areas above compare to last year's performance?

ACE YOUR NEW JOB

7 List the members of the company's executive board. These board members provide guidance and direction to the company and have a large impact on its success.

Name:

Title:

Key Qualifications (Credentials & Accomplishments):

Company Improvement Recommendations:

• • • • • • • • • • • • • • • • • •

Name:

Title:

Key Qualifications (Credentials & Accomplishments):

Company Improvement Recommendations:

• • • • • • • • • • • • • • • • • •

Name:

Title:

Key Qualifications (Credentials & Accomplishments):

Company Improvement Recommendations:

• • • • • • • • • • • • • • • • • • • •

Name:

Title:

Key Qualifications (Credentials & Accomplishments):

Company Improvement Recommendations:

• • • • • • • • • • • • • • • • • • • •

Name:

Title:

Key Qualifications (Credentials & Accomplishments):

Company Improvement Recommendations:

• • • • • • • • • • • • • • • • • • • •

Name:

Title:

Key Qualifications (Credentials & Accomplishments):

Company Improvement Recommendations:

Name:

Title:

Key Qualifications (Credentials & Accomplishments):

Company Improvement Recommendations:

8 What are the key risk factors or threats to the company's security and success? Note: Search for these within the narrative section.

Threats:

Summary:

9 List the company's top 3 competitors. You can also create a free account with Seeking Alpha, a site that provides content for financial markets, and search under "Peers" to see a list of competitors for many public companies. Visit: https://seekingalpha.com.

10 How is your company performing compared to its competitors, based on information in the narrative section. You may also refer to Seeking Alpha for additional information. Visit: https://seekingalpha.com.

6 TEAM INTERVIEWS WORKSHEET

The members of your team, as well as others with whom you collaborate, can be rich resources of information about the company and your role. Use LinkedIn (or the company website) along with this worksheet to deepen your understanding of them.

A. Profile Worksheet

1 Team Member 1:   Title:

Job Purpose:

Your Work Relationship to the Individual:

Brief Team Member Bio:

Team Member Education:

College 1:   Major:

College 2:   Major:

Prior Employment:

Company 1:   Title:

Company 2:   Title:

Company 3:   Title:

DEBORAH PINNOCK

People You Both Know (based on LinkedIn)

1. Contact Name:

2. Contact Name:

Hobbies in Common

1.   2.

• • • • • • • • • • • • • • • • • •

2 Team Member 2:   Title:

Job Purpose:

Your Work Relationship to the Individual:

Brief Team Member Bio:

Team Member Education:

College 1:   Major:

College 2:   Major:

Prior Employment:

Company 1:   Title:

Company 2:   Title:

Company 3:   Title:

People You Both Know (based on LinkedIn)

1. Contact Name:

2. Contact Name:

Hobbies in Common

1.   2.

ACE YOUR NEW JOB

3 Team Member 3:   Title:

Job Purpose:

Your Work Relationship to the Individual:

Brief Team Member Bio:

Team Member Education:

College 1:   Major:

College 2:   Major:

Prior Employment:

Company 1:   Title:

Company 2:   Title:

Company 3:   Title:

People You Both Know (based on LinkedIn)

1. Contact Name:

2. Contact Name:

Hobbies in Common

1.   2.

B. Interview Worksheet

A great way to get a deeper understanding of your new company and your role is to interview your co-workers, as well as individuals from other departments with whom you will be working. Keep in mind, you may only have 15 minutes or half hour to ask these questions. So, select the questions that will help you the most.

Questions About Their Experience in the Organization

- How long have you been with the organization?

- What do you like most about the company?

- What's an area in which the company is trying to improve? (Exercise good judgment in asking this)

- In your opinion what are the main challenges the company is currently facing?

- What have you found to be the best way to be successful in the company?

ACE YOUR NEW JOB

Questions to Get to Know Your Team Members or Managers better

- What would you say are some of your top strengths?

- Which of your strengths does the team rely on a lot?

- How would you describe your personality?

- What result would you like to achieve in your current role?

- Do you prefer to communicate via phone, email, text or face-to-face?

- Do you prefer meetings in the morning or afternoon?

- How would you describe your leadership style? (Recommended if interviewing your manager.)

- What would you like the team to achieve? (Recommended if interviewing your manager.)

- What are the top results you want this role to achieve? (Recommended if interviewing your manager.)

- If I have any questions, would you mind if I reached out to you?

Questions About Their Experience in Their Role
- What was your path to your current role?
- What do you like the most about your role?
- What do you find most challenging about your role and why?
- How do our roles interact?
- In your opinion, what qualities are needed to be successful in my role?
- What are some things I can do to make your job easier?

Questions About the Team
- What do you like the most about the team?
- What do you feel are the top strengths of the team?

- What skill set or experience would the team benefit from?

- What would you say is the biggest challenge the team is facing?

- What are your top tips to be an effective member of this team? (This question is good to ask both managers and peers.)

- What else do you think is helpful for me to know about the team?

7 OBSERVATION WORKSHEET

Nothing beats the power of observation. It includes what you are seeing, feeling and hearing. Analyzing these things can deepen your understanding of your role and company.
Very Important: This section is meant to be for your eyes only.

1 Company Culture

If your company was a person, how would you describe its personality? Friendly? Welcoming? Intimidating? High performing? Fun?

2 Manager Leadership Style

Leader 1 Name:
Dominant Leadership Style:

Leader 2 Name:
Dominant Leadership Style:

Kurt Lewin's Leadership Styles

- **Authoritarian** – This type of leader mostly makes decision without consulting or involving other people. Their preference is for others to follow their directives without question.
- **Democratic** – This type of leader consults others in their group or team on important decisions. They prefer to get input from their team and strive to lead by consensus.
- **Laissez-faire** – This type of leader may provide minimal guidance to the team members allowing a high level of autonomy and freedom for team members. They rely on team members to be self-directed.

ACE YOUR NEW JOB

3 Management Styles

Manager 1 Name:

Dominant Management Style:

Manager 2 Name:

Dominant Management Style:

Deborah Pinnock's Management Styles

- **Unaccountable Managers:** These managers consistently avoid taking ownership or accountability for the guidance provided to their team.
- **Micromanagers:** These managers may closely monitor or become deeply involved in the details of tasks they have assigned to their direct reports. They may become frustrated if their instructions or preferences are not followed precisely.
- **Vague Managers:** These managers may share broad project goals but provide minimal guidance.
- **Unresponsive Managers:** These managers are known for consistently not responding to their team members' communication, ignoring some or all questions or concerns.
- **Inexperienced Managers:** These managers may have excelled as individual contributors but struggle in the role of a people manager. This may be due to a lack of sufficient training.
- **People-Centric Managers:** These managers prioritize achieving results as well as the well-being of their team members, fostering a supportive and empowering environment for their team.

4 Colleague Assessment

Assess 3 colleagues with whom you work closely and rate them on a scale of 1-5 on the traits listed in the table below (1 being the lowest and 5 being the highest). See the next page for the definition of each trait.

Rating (1-5)

Colleague Name:
- Competent
- Helpful
- Trustworthy

Colleague Name:
- Competence
- Helpful
- Trustworthy

Colleague Name:
- Competence
- Helpful
- Trustworthy

Traits
- **Competent** - Knows and performs their job well
- **Helpful** - Willing to stop and explain something, provide assistance and meet with you on occasion
- **Trustworthy** - While trust must be earned, the person is not out to harm you professionally

5 Relationships:
Briefly describe the following relationships between:
Your manager and team

Your team members

Your manager and his/her peers

The members of the executive team, if you interact with them.

6 Meeting Behaviors

Level of timeliness for meetings
a) Most are early
b) Most are exactly on time
c) Most are late

Which statement(s) best describes meetings? You may select all that apply.
a) Meetings are held frequently
b) Meetings are well organized
c) Meetings are disorganized
d) Meetings are well organized and necessary
e) Meetings are disorganized and unnecessary

Do meetings typically use an agenda?

    Yes   No

7 Influencers

Whose ideas do people tend to like and listen to in meetings?

Whose permission do people seek for certain decisions? Note, this may not be the person with a leadership title.

Whose ideas tend to be ignored?

DEBORAH PINNOCK

8 Verbal Interactions

Provide a brief summary of the verbal interactions you have observed. For example, are people courteous and give each other time to complete their thoughts? Do folks give others appropriate credit? Do they have different meanings for certain words?

9 Attitudes

Describe the general attitudes you observe in meetings? Are participants upfront with their thoughts or guarded? Is there a freedom to share new ideas or not?

8
ROLE-RELATED SOFTWARE WORKSHEET

Most organizations provide their team members with various technology tools to help them be productive and efficient. An important step in training yourself is finding out which unique technology tools have been assigned to your role.

1 List the software needed to perform your role.

Software/App Name

Purpose

Help Desk Number/Link

Account Manager Name

Email / Phone Number

2 Software/App Name

Purpose

Help Desk Number/Link

Account Manager Name

Email / Phone Number

3 Software/App Name

Purpose

Help Desk Number/Link

Account Manager Name

Email / Phone Number

DEBORAH PINNOCK 31

9

E-LEARNING
WORKSHEET

E-learning is a great way to improve your skills in certain areas. Ask yourself the following questions to determine where you need to improve and how?

1 In which area do you feel the most insecure?

2 Which subject area do you need to master to excel in your role?

3 Which app or software do you need to improve in to excel in your role?

4 Which soft skill do you need to hone?

5 Does your job have an internal learning management system that's freely accessible to employees? If so, list its name.

ACE YOUR NEW JOB

6 If there is no internal learning management system, does the company have a contract with a third party learning organization where you can access learning at no cost? Which ones? For example, LinkedIn or Udemy?

7 Are there online learning platforms you can access through your local library? If you answered "yes", list the name of the platform.

Ace Your New Job Self-Assessment
Understanding Your Company, Your Role, & Your Colleagues

After completing the "Ace Your New Job" workbook and gaining knowledge about your company, answer the following questions to assess your understanding. Provide your response in the space provided.

1 What is the mission of the company? **5 points.**

2 What is the main product or service offered by your company? **5 points.**

3 Name one company highlight or achievement from the previous year. **5 points**

ACE YOUR NEW JOB

4 Who is the target market or audience that your company serves? **5 points.**

5 Name three main competitors of your company. **5 points.**

6 List three values of the company. **5 points.**

7 List two key clients or customers of your company. **5 points.**

8 How does your company make money? **5 points.**

9 Which professional platform can be used to learn about your colleagues' education, interests, and affiliations? **5 points.**

10 Write the names and titles of each member of your team. **5 points.**

11 What is the leadership style of your manager? **5 points.**

12 Identify two colleagues or individuals you will collaborate with in your new role. **5 points.**

13 Please list the name(s) of the manager(s) to whom you report. **5 points.**

ACE YOUR NEW JOB

14 List the top three duties of your role. **5 points.**

15 How does your role help the organization achieve its mission? **5 points.**

16 Based on the job description, what are three skills you should have? **5 points.**

17 List five key resources, based on the Ace Your New Job book and this workbook, that you can utilize to enhance your understanding of your organization. **5 points.**

18 Provide the name of one resource that offers insights into your company's financial performance for the previous year. **5 points.**

DEBORAH PINNOCK

19 How does your role interact or collaborate with two specific roles, either within your department or with other teams? **5 points.**

20 On a scale of 1-5 (1 being the lowest and 5 being the highest), how confident do you feel in your ability to excel in your role after completing the book and workbook? **5 points.**

TOTAL SCORE: _____ **/20**

Note: *This self-assessment is designed to gauge your current knowledge. Add up your total score and refer to the rubric. Use this assessment as a tool for self-reflection and to identify areas where you may want to seek further information or learning opportunities.*

ACE YOUR NEW JOB

Self-Assessment Rubric
Measure Your Progress Towards Mastery

Scoring Rubric:

70% - 79%

White Belt - You're a Rising Ace!

(Nice job! You've got the basics. Keep reviewing the workbook.)

80% - 89%

Blue Belt - The Proven Ace

(Good stuff! You're making great progress.)

90% - 100%

Red Belt- The Master Ace

(Fantastic! Now move from learning to adding value.)

DEBORAH PINNOCK

Reflections

What were the **most valuable resources** you discovered through this workbook?

_____
_____
_____
_____
_____
_____
_____
_____
_____
_____
_____

Reflections

How did the **resources you explored** deepen your knowledge of your new role?

Reflections

What are the **top insights** you learned through this process of self-training?

ACE YOUR NEW JOB

Reflections

How did the resources assist you in **developing relationships with your colleagues** and understanding their roles?

_____

_____

_____

_____

_____

_____

_____

_____

_____

_____

DEBORAH PINNOCK

Congratulations on completing the Ace Your New Job book and workbook!

Your proactive and driven approach as a professional is evident in both starting and finishing this brief journey. By investing your time and effort, you've established a strong foundation for success and growth in your current and future roles. Remember, your potential is limitless. Commit to continuous learning and take ownership of your professional growth. Maintain momentum by integrating daily reviews of the *Ace Your New Job* materials until the knowledge is internalized. All the best in this exciting new chapter of your work journey!

Deborah

ACE YOUR NEW JOB

Notes

Notes

Notes

About Deborah

Deborah Pinnock is a seasoned and respected career development specialist and coach with a passion for helping people recognize their value and equipping them to succeed in the workplace. Her career in the United States, which encompasses educational institutions and corporate organizations (including a Fortune 500 company), spans two decades. Within these industries, Deborah has held various roles involving teaching, training, employee engagement, corporate communication, marketing, sales, and customer service.

Her knowledge and experience, along with her certification as a Society of Human Resources Management (SHRM) certified professional, a John Maxwell Speaker, Trainer, and Coach, and her attainment of the Florida Soft Skills Credential, enable her to effectively equip and empower both new hires and seasoned individuals, to successfully navigate the complexities of the workplace. The mission of this Jamaican-born professional, who migrated to the US at a young age, is to utilize her journey to positively impact others.

Want to learn more?

Want to learn more about DebTalk, LLC, visit our website at https://debtalk.org/.

ACE YOUR NEW JOB